How to take your credit score from 0 to 800:

Tricks and tips to increase your credit score higher than you ever imagined

By

Joe Correa

COPYRIGHT

ACKNOWLEDGEMENTS

This book is dedicated to the people who want to make a better financial future for themselves and their family. It is my wish that you find the information in this book and use it to create the best possible credit.

How to take your credit score from 0 to 800:

Tricks and tips to increase your credit score higher than you ever imagined

By

Joe Correa

TABLE OF CONTENTS

Chapter 10: How to Apply For a Home Mortgage and Get Approved

Chapter 11: How to Qualify For Credit When You Have No Credit At All

Chapter 12: Real Life Example of Someone Who Increased Their Credit Score to Over 800 Starting From Having No Credit At All

Credit Score Myths

Credit Vocabulary

INTRODUCTION

How to take your credit score from 0 to 800: Tricks and tips to increase your credit score higher than you ever imagined

By Joe Correa

If you want to increase your credit score to the highest it's ever been, you found the right book!

Why do some people have low credit scores while others have high scores? Why are some people constantly denied credit while others always approved? These are common questions that can be answered with one word, "knowledge".

You will learn how to:

- Get approved for credit cards.
- Get approved for a car loan.
- Have a better chance at getting a job.
- Prevent having to put deposits on new accounts and having lower down payments.
- Finance your home with the best interest rates.
- Apply for any loan with confidence.

If you know what to do to increase your score, you will prevent making mistakes most people make on their credit.

Having a high credit score can benefit you in so many ways. It can change your life completely.

How can you increase your credit score and be able to finance what you want at the best rates? The tips and tricks in this book will help you to use tools that are currently available to you but most people don't even know about.

If you want to have a successful financial life, you need to learn how to use credit to your benefit and this is only possible through a high credit score. Don't wait to get denied on applications to take your credit seriously, start now by reading and learning what is necessary to take your credit from 0 to 800.

ABOUT THE AUTHOR

For many years I have helped people to finance a home or to lower their payments. I have worked for different banks, lenders, and an investment advisory firm. I began as a college math professor at Miami-Dade Community College teaching all subjects I was required to teach at age 23, which was kind of awkward for many of my students since most of them were around my age or older but my ability to teach others and to master math helped me make difficult subjects become easier to understand. I was approached by Union Planters Bank which is now Regions Bank to work for them as a Financial Advisor. On a daily basis, I was required to open the bank doors, open the bank vault, open personal and business bank accounts, complete home equity lines of credit and home equity loans, and many other tasks. I especially enjoyed closing home equity loans and wanted to learn more so I got my mortgage license and went to work for a mortgage company. A year later I started my own mortgage company and soon transitioned to a correspondent lender. I was able to help hundreds of people to buy a home, refinance to lower payments, and to take cash out to pay off debts or reinvest. When the economy slowed down and banks stopped lending I decided to focus on helping others by educating. I hope this book reaches as many people as possible and helps shape a new future for many that might feel stranded on their own without a solution.

CHAPTER 1

Understanding Your Credit Score

CREDIT SCORE DETERMINATION

Your credit score is determined by five main categories which are:

1. Payment history
2. Credit utilization
3. Length of credit history
4. New credit and inquiries
5. Credit mix

1. **Payment history** accounts for approximately 35% of your credit score which is a high percentage. It can be determined by seeing how often a borrower has made payments on time. The repayment of debt in the past is the best way to determine future payments. If you often make late payments, you will probably continue to make late payments. If you often make payments on time, you will probably continue to do the same. The larger the debt payment is, the greater importance it has. If you have a credit card payment of $100 every month and make payments on time but you are often late on

your mortgage payment which has a payment of $2,300, your score will be more negatively affected by the late payments. Making payments on time every month will gradually increase your credit score and will make it easier for you to obtain credit in the future.

2. **Credit utilization** accounts for about 30% of your credit score which is almost a third of your score. It will determine how much of your available credit you are using and if you have no available debt to draw from. Credit utilization is an important factor as it shows just how well you are doing financially. For example, if you have a credit limit of $5,000 and owe $500 you would be using only 10% of your available credit. If you have a credit limit of $10,000 and owe $8,000, you would be using 80% of your available credit. Ideally, you want to use between 25 – 35% of your available credit and no higher. This does not mean you need to owe 25 – 35% or less to have the best possible chance at a good credit score. This will simply improve your score. You don't necessarily need to carry debt to see you credit score rise. You can always pay off your card every time you owe money. Often borrowers that want to see an increase in their credit scores often pay down debt so that it is below 35% of what you have available. Paying off debt completely will have an even greater

benefit on your overall credit score as it will increase your available credit.

3. **Length of credit history** accounts for 15% of your total credit score. This basically determines how old your credit is based on all the accounts that are still open. If you want your credit score to be high, you need to make payments for a longer period of time. People who have recently opened a credit card account will not see a significant rise in their score. New credit will not get you higher scores. You need to make payments for a while to see a gradual increase. Make sure to maintain accounts that you have had open for a long period of time open, as this will benefit you as time goes by (Don't close your oldest accounts!). For example, if you close a credit account, you lose whatever payment history you created so you want to make sure you don't close your older credit accounts. Paying off a debt is not considered closing it. If you have a credit card on which you have made payments on time for a period of 3 years and then has been paid off, you don't necessarily have to close it. You can keep this account open and only use that credit card when you need it.

4. **New credit and inquiries** account for 10% of your overall credit score. Borrowers who are applying for credit cards often will see a drop in their score

initially. Avoid applying for too many credit accounts at a time so that your score stays high and only has brief moments when it goes down. Every time you apply for credit your credit report will show an inquiry. An inquiry is when a bank pulls your credit history to see how you have made payments in the past and other relevant information before making a decision on your credit application. Having too many inquiries will lower your credit score but will never be the only reason a bank will not lend you money.

5. **Credit mix** accounts for 10% of your score and can affect your capacity to increase your overall credit score. Having a mix of credit accounts means that you have different types of credit such as: car loans, credit cards, home loans (mortgages), department store credit cards, student loans, etc. Having one credit card and one car loan means you have a mix of different types of credit. This does not mean you have to run out and get as many different types of debt as possible to increase your credit score. You should only apply for what you need and what will benefit you. You don't need to have any specific type of credit account to increase your credit score. Some people can have a 750 credit score without ever having more than just credit cards.

These 5 categories: payment history, credit utilization, length of credit history, new credit and inquiries, credit mix, all play an important role in determining your credit score. Knowing how to manage them will make all the difference when improving your credit. They each weigh on your credit in different ways so make sure to focus first on the ones that will affect your credit the most. Payment history and credit utilization together account for 65% of your credit score. For this reason, it's a good idea to always make payments on time and not owe more than a certain amount on them. Doing these two things will increase your credit score fast and will keep it high as long as continue to follow this pattern of paying on time and not owing more than 35% of what is available to you in credit. Remember, this means maintaining your debt below 35% of your total available credit on all your credit accounts. This includes credit cards, car loans, mortgages, etc. For most people, simply controlling your credit card debt to stay beneath 35% of what your available credit balance is, will play a major role in managing their credit score.

For example, if you have debts on your credit report and you want to figure out if you are below 35% of your credit utilization rate, you can simple add up all the debt you have and then divide this number by the total amount of credit you have available on all your accounts. This can be easy to calculate and is useful information when you don't know where you stand credit wise.

Total debts

Credit card 1: $1,200

Credit card 2: $4,200

Car loan: $13,000

Total debt: $18,400

Total Limits on each account:

Credit card 1: $2,000

Credit card 2: $10,000

Car loan: $30,000

Total credit limits: $42,000

Total debts/ total of credit limits

$18,400/$42,000 = 43.8%

43.8% is higher than where we need to be which is: 35%, so you need to make a few changes to get below 35%.

One solution could be to pay off all of your credit cards. This would give us a new total debt of $13,000 but we would still have the same credit limits.

If you paid off your credit cards, your debt to credit limit ratio would look like this:

$13,000/$42,000 = 30.1%

By paying off your credit cards, you were able to bring down your credit utilization rate down below 35% which will allow you to improve your credit score. You can also lower what you owe on your car loan and create the same effect but it would be a wiser decision to pay off the credit cards instead simply because they normally carry a higher interest rate.

CHAPTER 2

How Do You Know If You Have a Good Credit Score?

This can be a difficult question to answer if you don't know what your ultimate goal is. If you are applying for a credit card, you might not need a very high credit score but if you are applying for a home loan you will want to have a credit score as high as possible to reduce the interest rate you end up getting which will lower the amount of interest you pay over the life of the loan. Let's go over different credit score ranges to see what each is considered.

CREDIT SCORE RANGES

Credit scores fall into different ranges. Most banks and lenders check to see in which range you are in to determine if they grant you credit or not and at what interest rate. In general, having a low credit score is always better than having no credit score and having a high credit score is better than having a low credit score. By comparing different credit score ranges you can determine if you have good credit or bad credit. Remember, you will learn some tricks to quickly improve your credit score later on in this book so don't get discouraged when you see each of the ranges.

Credit scores range from 300 to 850 with 300 being the lowest and 850 being the highest.

Fico credit score ranges are:

850 – 800 is considered excellent

799 – 740 is considered very good

739 – 670 is considered good

669 – 580 is considered fair

579 – 300 is considered poor

Most people fall into one of these categories but a few have no credit score at all. Having no credit score will result in not getting credit at all. Later on you will learn how to easily obtain a credit score.

People who have a credit score between 850 – 800 will commonly be approved for credit. They will usually get approved for the best rates from the strictest banks.

People who have a credit score between 799 – 740 will get excellent to good rates and will normally get approved for loans without many restrictions as they have a high probability of paying back loans, historically and statistically speaking.

People who have a credit score between 739 – 670 have a good probability of paying back a loan so they are often granted credit and will receive good to average rates.

People who have a credit score between 669 – 580 will normally have a medium to low probability of paying back a loan and will be approved credit on a case by case basis. When they are approved for credit, rates are usually high.

People who have a credit score between 579 – 300 will usually not get approved for credit at all unless a security deposit is made in advance. Even with a security deposit, rates will be high.

NOTE:

Not being in any of these credit score ranges is a problem since you won't be considered for credit at all because there is no way to calculate your probability of paying back a loan. Make sure you have a credit score before applying for a loan.

WHO ARE THE THREE MAIN CREDIT REPORTING AGENCIES AND WHAT DO THEY DO?

The three credit bureaus

There are three credit bureaus that report your fico score which are Experian®, Transunion®, and Equifax®. Each reports what is known as a FICO score which was created by the Fair Isaac Corporation. The Fair Isaac Corporation specializes in "predictive analytics" which means they try to predict how you will make future payments. They take information and analyze it to predict what could happen.

Essentially, you will have three credit scores and each credit grantor will choose what credit bureau to pull credit from and see what you fico score is for that specific credit bureau. You will not be able to choose which one they review but you can take the necessary steps to improve your credit to the point that it does not matter what credit bureau they review. Credits scores from all three credit bureaus show up as numbers like this: 720 734 740. Experian might report a 720 credit score, while Equifax reports a 734 score, and Transunion a 740 score.

Most banks only check one credit score when you apply for credit card or car loan but will check all three when applying for a mortgage. For this reason, applying for a mortgage at many banks can lower your credit scores fast since they will review all three credit bureaus versus applying for a credit card which will only lower one score.

Make sure you have a credit score for each credit bureau, as in some cases you will find you only have one or two credit scores simply because a bank or lender did not report your payment history to all of the credit reporting agencies. You would be surprised how often this happens and how often people are denied credit due to this technical error. Never assume banks will report information accurately, even though they should. Always review your credit report and make sure information is reflected correctly so that you can benefit from this in the future and prevent being denied for a loan.

CHAPTER 3

How to Read and Interpret Your Credit Report

WHERE CAN YOU GET A COPY OF YOUR CREDIT REPORT?

In order to read and interpret your credit report you need to have a copy of it first. You can order a free copy of your credit report at http://www.annualcreditreport.com/. You are entitled to one free credit report every 12 months which has been determined by federal law. You are also entitled to a copy of your credit report whenever you have been denied credit or if you have had any adverse credit action taken against you. The bank or company that denied credit should provide you with instructions as to how to obtain a copy of your credit report for free. Most websites will charge a fee for your credit report. If you only want to see one of the credit bureaus, this fee will be lower. If you want to see your credit information for all three credit bureaus, the fee will be higher. Make sure you request a complete credit report with all three of your credit scores as, as the difference in cost might be minimal and will be very useful. Remember, the three credit bureaus you want to have information on are Equifax®, Experian®, and Transunion®.

Take your time and go over your credit report in detail to make sure all the information on it is reflected accurately.

How to read your credit report

PERSONAL INFORMATION

Personal information is usually used to identify you when reviewing your credit in order to prevent fraud and identity theft.

Names associated:

John Doe

John B. Doe

John Benjamin Doe

These are examples of all the names you have used when applying for credit or any other reason someone has reviewed your credit for, including: mortgage application, rental application, credit card application, school financing, etc.

Addresses associated:

123 Happy Street Apt 17

Orlando, FL 32811

123 Red Robin Lane

Kansas City, Mo 64030

567 Blue Jay Street

Atlanta, GA 30301

These are all the addresses you could have entered on past credit applications.

Other personal information:

Social Security Number Variations

XXX-XX-1234

XXX-XX-1224

XXX-XX-1233

These are all the social security numbers you could have entered in the past when applying for credit. Obviously, only one should be the correct number that was entered when applying for credit.

Year of birth

1976

This is the year of birth you have entered when applying for credit.

Telephone Number(s)

123-234-3456

123-234-1111

These are all the past phone numbers you have when entered on a credit application.

Past or current employers

ABC Corporation

123 Corporation

These are all the employers you have worked for and have entered on credit applications or past employers that have reviewed your credit report when applying for work.

Remarks: A fraud alert has been placed on the credit report. Contact customer before granting credit or when credit is requested.

Remarks are often comments that you or a creditor have requested to appear on your credit report. Fraud and identity theft comments are the most common and are important to have in case someone has stolen your wallet or personal information.

PUBLIC RECORDS

Bankruptcy Chapter 7

Filing date: 05/22/2010

Identifying number: 4154124

Court: Southern District of Georgia

Amount: $433,928

Judgement

Filing date: 01/01/2008

Identifying number: CF123456

Court: ABC County Magistrate

Plaintiff: NML

Amount: $300

These are types of negative public records that can appear on your credit report and will normally provide complete details as to your past or current situation.

ACCOUNTS

These usually show up as open or closed accounts. Open accounts are all the accounts you have and are available for use including credit cards. When accounts are closed for any reason they will appear under the list of closed accounts.

Open Installment Accounts:

Account name: ABC Mortgage

Contact information: 123 Four Corners Street

Tallahassee, FL 32301

Account #: 1234XXXXXXX

Account type: Real estate

Current balance: $392,450

Credit limit: $450,000

High Balance: $450,000

Monthly payment: $2,850

Date opened: 11/08/2015

Account status: Open

Payment Status: Current

Payment history: If paid on time, "OK" will appear for all the months payment was made on time. You should see a calendar for all of the months for which the account has been open and a box with a short notice of payment below the general account information. In most cases it will show "OK" but if you pay late after 30 days, 60 days, or 90 days, it will state this instead.

Open Revolving Accounts:

Account name: Bank of XYZ

Contact information: 45 Belmont St

Los Angeles, CA 90005

Account #: 1233333XXXXXXXXX

Account type: Credit card

Current balance: $3,156

Credit limit: $10,000

High Balance: $4,210

Monthly payment: $185

Minimum Payment: $35

Date opened: 04/11/2007

Account status: Open

Payment Status: Current

Payment history: If paid on time, "OK" will appear for all the months payment was made on time. You should see a calendar for all of the months for which the account has been open and a box with a short notice of payment below the general account information. In most cases it will show "OK" but if you pay late after 30 days, 60 days, or 90 days, it will state this instead.

Closed Account:

Account name: Bank of ABC

Contact information: 4007 Wine Country Street

Seattle, WA 98146

Account #: 777131XXXXXXXXX

Account type: Credit card

Current balance: $0

Credit limit: $3,500

High Balance: $0

Monthly payment: $0

Minimum Payment: $0

Date opened: 04/11/2007

Account status: Closed, Paid Satisfactorily

Payment Status: Closed

Payment history: If paid on time, "OK" will appear for all the months payment was made on time. You should see a calendar for all of the months for which the account has been open and a box with a short notice of payment below the general account information. In most cases it will show "OK" but if you pay late after 30 days, 60 days, or 90 days, it will state this instead.

Negative Account/Collections:

Account name: ABC Electricity Company

Contact information: P.O. Box 555233

Seattle, WA 98146

Account #: 9144XXXXXXXXX

Account type: Collection Agency

Current balance: $90

Credit limit: $250

High Balance: $0

Monthly payment: $0

Minimum Payment: $0

Date opened: 04/11/2007

Account status: Seriously past due date, assigned to collection agency

Payment Status: Failed to pay

Payment history: If paid on time, "OK" will appear for all the months payment was made on time. For late payment accounts and collections, you will see different colored boxes for the degree of lateness. You should see a calendar for all of the months for which the account has been open and a box with a short notice of payment, in this case it will show "OK" for some months but will show 30, 60, 90, 120, 150, and then a "C" for when it became a collection.

CREDIT INQUIRIES

Credit inquiries will show up on your credit report when you have applied for credit or when you have allowed a company to review your credit report. All of the times you reviewed your own credit report will not affect you negatively (your credit score will not drop for this reason) but will still reflect on your credit report.

Credit inquiries made by others:

Account name: ABC Bank

Inquiry date: 06-07-2008

Contact information: P.O. Box 999231

Seattle, WA 98146

Account name: XYZ Leasing

Inquiry date: 03-22-2006

Contact information: P.O. Box 333421

Tallahassee, FL 32301

Credit inquiries made by you:

Account name: Equifax® Credit

Inquiry date: 09/28/2011

MEDICAL INFORMATION

If any medical information such as collections or amounts due to a medical institution can appear here as well as the negative account information section of the credit report.

CHAPTER 4

How Your Credit Score Affects Your Life

Your credit score can have a significant effect on your financial life over time. By having bad, good, average, or great credit you will end up having low payments or high payments on purchases you finance.

Good credit = low interest rates and lower interest payments

Bad credit = high interest rates and higher interest payments

Over time, making lower interest payments will mean you will have more cash left over to use for other purposes instead of giving it to the bank.

If the purchase is large, such as a house, this payment can be almost double when you have bad credit which will mean you will end up paying much more interest over time than someone who has great credit. Smaller debts, such as a credit card, can affect you even more when you have bad credit because you will get approved for high interest rates which will mean you will have higher interest payments. If you have bad credit, you might not get approved for specific purchase benefit programs that include points, miles, or cash back offers. Some cards will require that you secure the credit card with money you deposit in a bank account. These credit cards are called "secured credit cards". Having good credit is important and can be easily obtained by most people who are able to manage their debts in a responsible manner and manage their credit intelligently. By seeing how significant the difference is when you have great, good, average, and bad credit, you will understand why you will benefit much more when you have a high credit score.

Often, being in a specific credit score range will mean having a particular interest rate so you want to know what ranges are ideal and what ranges you want to stay away from. For example, if you have a 650 credit score you would be in between a 620 – 660 credit score range which would be below average. Each bank determines what score ranges you need to be in or above to be granted credit.

Let's go over different examples so that you can compare different payments based on different payment terms.

If you have a credit score 620 or below this is how much it would cost you to finance your car and home purchase

For the purchase of a home this would be a possible payment scenario based on a credit score of 620 or below if you are granted a loan:

Home loan amount: $200,000

Interest rate: 5.8%

Term: 30 years

Payment amount: $1,174

Total interest paid over 30 years: $222,462

An ideal situation with a great credit score would be:

Home loan amount: $200,000

Interest rate: 4%

Term: 30 years

Payment amount: $955

Total interest paid over 30 years: $143,739

For the purchase of a car this would be a possible payment scenario based on a credit score of 620 or below if you are granted a loan:

Car loan amount: $18,000

Interest rate: 11%

Term: 5 years

Payment amount: $391

An ideal situation with a great credit score would be:

Car loan amount: $18,000

Interest rate: 2%

Term: 6 years

Payment amount: $266

THE FINAL RESULT

Even though the difference in mortgage payments is only $219 more every month, the total interest paid over 30 years is $78,723 more because you had a lower credit score.

On your car purchase, you would be paying $125 more every month in loan payments because you have a lower credit. If you had a great credit score you could have a lower interest rate and would have the option to finance the loan for 6 years instead of 5 years which would lower your monthly payments.

If you have a credit score between 620 and 680 this is how much it would cost you to finance a car and a house

For the purchase of a home this would be a possible payment scenario based on a credit score between 620 and 680 if you are granted a loan:

Home loan amount: $200,000

Interest rate: 5.6%

Term: 30 years

Payment amount: $1,148

Total interest paid over 30 years: $213,337

An ideal situation with a great credit score would be:

Home loan amount: $200,000

Interest rate: 4%

Term: 30 years

Payment amount: $955

Total interest paid over 30 years: $143,739

For the purchase of a car this would be a possible payment scenario based on a credit score between 620 and 680 if you are granted a loan:

Car loan amount: $18,000

Interest rate: 8%

Term: 5 years

Payment amount: $365

An ideal situation with a great credit score would be:

Car loan amount: $18,000

Interest rate: 2%

Term: 6 years

Payment amount: $266

THE FINAL RESULT

Even though the difference in mortgage payments is only $193 more every month, the total interest paid over 30 years is $69,598 more because you had a lower credit score than the ideal score.

On your car purchase, you would be paying $99 more every month in loan payments because you have a lower credit score. If you had a great credit score you could have a lower interest rate and would have the option to finance the loan for up to 6 years instead of 5 years which would lower your monthly payments.

If you have a credit score between 680 and 720 this is how much it would cost you to finance a car and a house

For the purchase of a home this would be a possible payment scenario based on a credit score between 680 and 720 if you are granted a loan:

Home loan amount: $200,000

Interest rate: 4.65%

Term: 30 years

Payment amount: $1,031

Total interest paid over 30 years: $171,259

An ideal situation with a great credit score would be:

Home loan amount: $200,000

Interest rate: 4%

Term: 30 years

Payment amount: $955

Total interest paid over 30 years: $143,739

For the purchase of a car this would be a possible payment scenario based on a credit score between 680 and 720 if you are granted a loan:

Car loan amount: $18,000

Interest rate: 6%

Term: 6 years

Payment amount: $298

An ideal situation with a great credit score would be:

Car loan amount: $18,000

Interest rate: 2%

Term: 6 years

Payment amount: $266

THE FINAL RESULT

Even though the difference in mortgage payments is only $76 more every month, the total interest paid over 30 years is $27,520 more because you had a lower credit score than the ideal score.

On your car purchase, you would be paying $32 more every month in loan payments because you have a lower credit score. If you had a great credit score you could have a lower interest rate and would have the option to finance the loan for up to 6 years instead of 5 years which would lower your monthly payments.

If you have a credit score between 720 and 760 this is how much it would cost you to finance a car and a house

For the purchase of a home this would be a possible payment scenario based on a credit score between 720 and 760 if you are granted a loan:

Home loan amount: $200,000

Interest rate: 4.25%

Term: 30 years

Payment amount: $984

Total interest paid over 30 years: $154,197

An ideal situation with a great credit score would be:

Home loan amount: $200,000

Interest rate: 4%

Term: 30 years

Payment amount: $955

Total interest paid over 30 years: $143,739

For the purchase of a car this would be a possible payment scenario based on a credit score between 720 and 760 if you are granted a loan:

Car loan amount: $18,000

Interest rate: 4%

Term: 7 years

Payment amount: $246

An ideal situation with a great credit score would be:

Car loan amount: $18,000

Interest rate: 2%

Term: 7 years

Payment amount: $230

THE FINAL RESULT

Even though the difference in mortgage payments is only $29 more every month, the total interest paid over 30 years is $10,458 more.

On your car purchase, you would be paying $16 more every month in loan payments because you have a lower credit score than the ideal. If you had a very high credit score you could have a lower interest rate and would have the option to finance the loan for up to 7 years which would lower your monthly payments.

Make sure to use a reasonable financing time period as your car will continue to loss value over time. The longer the financing time term the more problems this will bring you in the future. The ideal time frame to finance a car is no more than 60 months.

If you have a credit score above 760 this is how much it would cost you to finance a car and a house

For the purchase of a house this would be a possible payment scenario based on a credit score of 760 or higher:

Home loan amount: $200,000

Interest rate: 4%

Term: 30 years

Payment amount: $955

Total interest paid over 30 years: $143,739

For the purchase of a car this would be a possible payment scenario based on a credit score of 760 or higher:

Car loan amount: $18,000

Interest rate: 2%

Term: 7 years

Payment amount: $230

THE FINAL RESULT

You will see that by having the highest credit score possible or in this example anything above 760, you will get the lowest interest rate and longest payment term option. This will give you the lowest monthly payment which will save you the most money when it comes to getting a loan and paying interest over a specific time frame. Some loan programs require an over 800 credit score which can also be a great situation to be in if you qualify.

NOTE: Some mortgage and car loan programs offer lower interest rates but may have adjustable rates or costs involved. Make sure to always read the fine print before signing any documents.

CHAPTER 5

Tricks and Tips You Can Do to Instantly Increase Your Credit Score

There are many ways to improve your credit score fast. Each has its own set of factors that will help you increase your credit score in no time.

Some of the best ways to increase your credit score are:

1. **Request for a credit line increase** on your credit cards. Assume you owe $2,800 on a $3,000 and don't have the money to pay it off in full or at least pay it down to 35% of what the credit limit is. You can always call your bank and ask for a credit line increase. If they ask you by how much you would like to request to have the credit line increase, make sure to estimate three times what you owe so that you are around 30% of what you have to pay back. Let's say you owe $3,000, you need to request $9,000 which would be an increase of $6,000. This way if you are approved for $8,000, you will owe 35% or less of what your credit limit is which will immediately improve your credit score. This won't cost you anything but the bank will often need to check your credit in order to do this. Remember, the

purpose of increasing your credit line is not to go deeper into debt, but to improve your credit score.

2. **Paying off a credit card** or paying down a credit card, car loan, or mortgage so that you're credit utilization rate is below 35%. This can often be easier to do with smaller debts that have low balances but will still positively improve your credit score. Lowering your credit utilization rate even if it's not below 35% will still improve your credit but the lower it is the better it will be for you. For example, if you owe $1,500 on a credit card that has a $2,000 credit limit and you pay it off, this will mean you now have $2,000 available in credit instead of $500. For this reason, your score should go up.

3. **Paying your bills on time** can have the greatest positive effect on your credit report. Make sure you always pay a few days in advance of the due date to prevent any delays in payment which could affect your credit. Never choose to make the payment exactly on the due date as there are always things that can delay the payment such as bank holidays, slow mail delivery, payment processing, etc.

4. **Request to have incorrect credit information removed** including inquiries (credit checks), late payments, incorrect account opening history, accounts that are not yours, and incorrect amounts owed on different accounts. Sometimes credit

reporting agencies will report inaccurate information on your credit report that needs to be corrected. People who have similar names to yours can have one of their debts on your credit report. Other times, a family member with the same name can have your information on their credit report. Credit inquiries can appear for credit applications that you did not make or did not approve to be processed. A late payment can appear on your credit report when you made your payments on time. These situations are all reasons to dispute incorrect information on your credit report.

5. **Get a secured credit card** to create a new account. When a credit card is secured, it basically means you will be putting your money in a bank account and will be allowed to use the same amount in the form of credit on a credit card. If you have not been approved for a credit card in the past, this is a great way to build credit and increase your credit score.

6. **Stop using credit to pay for things.** This a great way to take a more proactive approach towards your finances in general. Not owing more money will immediately increase your capacity to pay off or pay down debt which will increase your credit scores. Don't continue down the pay of accumulating debt with the purpose of obtaining or improving your credit score. Small debts managed intelligently and

paid on time will allow you to have a higher credit score.

7. **Ask a family member or close friend to add you as an authorized signer on their credit card.** This can have a very positive effect on your credit if your friend or family member makes their payments on time every month and carries little to no debt on it. Whatever is reflected on their credit report for that account will now reflect on your credit report which will ultimately increase your credit score in no time. This is a powerful and effective way to improve your credit. Make sure they continue to make their payments on time. If they will be late on their payments, they need to let you know in advance so you can request to be removed from the account. This will prevent you from having negative information on your credit report.

8. **Apply for a credit card with the intention of not using it.** For most people, this will not make any sense at all but it's quite simple. In order to improve your credit score you need to have more credit available without increasing debt. For this reason, you can apply for a credit card and be approved for a credit limit of $5,000 which will increase your total available credit by $5,000. This will lower your debt to credit limit ratio which is one of the main factors used by credit bureaus when calculating your credit

score. Make sure this credit card does not have any fees, especially annual fees, or else you will accumulate unwanted expenses. Put this card away so that you don't use it at all. It's much easier to forget you have the card than to resist the temptation to use it.

CHAPTER 6

How to Dispute Incorrect Information on Your Credit Report

Credit repair companies normally use a number of tools to improve your credit scores. One of the most effective tools they use to improve someone's credit is by disputing and updating incorrect or invalid information on your credit report. Doing this can benefit you in many ways. Besides improving your credit scores, it will allow banks and lenders to appropriately assess your financial situation when deciding whether or not to grant you credit.

Reasons why you should dispute information on your credit report are:

- Incorrect payment amounts are shown on your credit report.
- Accounts that are not yours show up on your credit report.
- Inquiries you did not authorize.
- Incorrect address shows up on your credit report.
- Incorrect employment information.
- Credit limits are wrong for some accounts.
- A car payment you make is not showing up on your credit report.

- Derogatory (negative) information on the credit report that should be removed.
- Your name is spelled incorrectly.

When should derogatory (negative) information be removed from your credit report?

- Late payments stay on your credit report for 7 years from the date in which it was first late.
- Collections stay on your credit report for 7 years from when the account was first late.
- A chapter 7 bankruptcy stays on your credit report for 10 years from the filing date.
- A chapter 13 bankruptcy stays on your credit report for 7 years from the filing date.
- Credit inquiries are removed from your credit report after 2 years from when credit was applied.
- Unpaid tax liens remain for 10 years on your credit report if not paid.
- Paid tax liens remain for 7 years on your credit report once they are paid.
- Civil judgements stay on your credit report for 7 years from the date they are filed.

These are all valid reasons to dispute information on your credit report especially when certain things should have been removed automatically. Negative information needs to be removed by the time frames established by law. For example, if you have a credit inquiry still showing from 4 years ago (after 2 years it should automatically be removed), it needs to be removed and you can have this done by disputing it.

Ways to dispute credit report information

Knowing how to dispute incorrect information or adding correct information will make the most difference when trying to improve your credit or at least having accurate information reflecting on your credit report.

Disputing or correcting invalid information on your credit report can be done in three ways:

1. Physical letters sent over the mail
2. Via each one of the credit bureaus websites.
3. Via the phone by calling each one of the credit bureaus.

Advantages and disadvantages of each one

*Advantages of disputing information on your credit report via **physical mail**:*

- When you send documents over the mail you have physical proof it was sent and somebody has to pick up your letter and read it.
- When it is received over the mail, you can have delivery confirmation so that you know when it was received.
- It's easier to personalize physical letters.

Disadvantages of disputing information on your credit report via physical mail:

- Physical mail can sometimes get lost unless you pay extra for a delivery confirmation service.
- Physical mail can get mixed up with other papers when it is received by a customer service representative.
- Physical mail takes longer to arrive and may take longer to get an answer back which will mean that any updates will be delayed. You won't be able to speed things up in case you are in a hurry to correct information on your credit report.

*Advantages of disputing information on your credit report via the credit bureaus **website**:*

- When you dispute information online you save time and money.
- Disputing information online allows you to have simple and clear options to choose from which are most relevant to the credit bureau when making decisions whether or not to make the changes requested.
- Submitting your dispute online through one of the credit bureaus websites will speed up the process which will allow you to get an answer sooner than over physical mail.

Disadvantages of disputing information on your credit report via the credit bureaus website:

- Some of the websites might not have certain options which are pertinent to your particular situation.
- Disputing information online might not offer the option to tell your story as some situations might require a lengthy explanation of what is going on.
- Submitting disputes online is less personalized than other methods.

Advantages of disputing information on your credit report over the **phone**:

- When you dispute information over the phone you are able to speak to an actual person.
- Disputing information over the phone allows you to explain your situation no matter how lengthy it might be.
- In some cases, changes will be done immediately when requested over the phone which will save you a lot of time.

Disadvantages of disputing information on your credit report over the phone:

- When disputing information over the phone, you will often have long waiting periods in order to speak to an actual person as well as the time spent on the automated services to direct you to the right department.
- When you speak to a customer service representative, you could be asked to provide proof of your claims or requests for corrected information on your credit report over the mail which will delay the process.
- When calling over the phone you are limited to speaking to a representative during business hours only.

Each of these can be effective but the difference in time can be longer when doing everything over the mail. If you are in a rush to improve your credit, choose the website route first and if you don't get the response you want move on to trying the phone or physical mail options.

SAMPLE DISPUTE LETTER MADE TO A CREDIT REPORTING AGENCY

Date:

Your name:

Your address:

Credit bureau name:

Credit bureau address:

Attn: Dispute department

RE: Dispute request

While reviewing my credit report several things appeared that are not accurate that I would like to have corrected.

1. The "XYZ" credit card account 12344XXXXXX shows that I owe $3,432 but it should show a zero balance since it has been paid off. This account needs to show a zero balance.

2. There is an account that is not mine but shows up on my credit report. This account needs to be removed:

"XXX" credit card company account number 1234XXXXXXXX.

Please make the necessary corrections and on my credit report as soon as possible. I have attached a statement for "XYZ" credit card showing I do not have a balance on it any more.

Should you have any questions you can contact me at 123-432-2234.

Sincerely,

"Your Name"

Before sending the letter call each credit reporting agency and ask them to confirm you have the correct mailing address for their dispute department. Also ask them if you need to include your social security number on the letter as this is sometimes requested.

To dispute information on your credit online, you can find each of the credit bureaus by going to:

Experian®

www.experian.com/disputes/main.html

Transunion®

https://www.transunion.com/credit-disputes/dispute-your-credit

Equifax®

https://www.equifax.com/personal/disputes

For physical mail and phone contact information

You will find additional contact information such as phone numbers and mailing addresses by going to each of the credit bureau websites in case you would like to dispute information over the phone and through the mail. Phone numbers and mailing addresses some times change so you need to make sure you go online to find the most up to date information for each of the credit bureaus.

CHAPTER 7

Owing Versus Paying Off Debt

For many people, this is a question often made every time the bill arrives. Should I make my minimum payment, complete payment, or pay it off? When you understand how debt works and how compound interest can make things much worse, you will have no doubt as to what needs to be done. Compound interest is also known as "interest on interest" which basically means that once you start making minimum payments instead of principal and interest, you will begin to pay interest on the interest you did not pay the preceding month. Interest on interest grows rapidly to the point that you start to increase debt instead of eliminating it. For this reason, stay away from paying interest on interest by paying down your debt every month and never choose to make minimum payments. Your goal should not be to carry debt from month to month but rather to pay it down whenever possible. If you carry debt you will have to pay interest and paying interest only benefits the bank.

Is it better to carry debt or to pay off what you owe, in order to improve your credit score?

A larger portion of the general population carries debt month to month without paying it off which can have a positive or negative effect on their credit. For some people, carrying debt and paying on time every month should mean their credit score will go up because of the positive payment history they are creating. For other people, carrying debt could mean they are increasing the amount of debt they have which will lower the amount of credit they have available to use. This will lower your credit score when you reach a certain amount or percentage. Most credit bureaus suggest that you stay below 35% of what your credit limit is.

For example, if you have a credit limit of $10,000, stay below $3,500 in debt. This is not a rule but it helps to stay below this number in general.

Should I pay off of my debt all at once or should I pay it down gradually?

Let's say you have a particular future event, like applying for a mortgage, where you need your credit score to increase fast and by a large percentage. This would be the perfect situation to pay off all of your debts as you will see a large increase in your credit score the following month or two. Knowing that you will need this increase makes it the perfect opportunity to use this pay off strategy instead of paying it off slowly.

When you're not in a rush, paying down your debt gradually will allow you to slowly increase your credit score every time you make a monthly payment. This is another good strategy as long as you are paying down your debt which will benefit your score when you pay on time and when you lower the percentage you owe on your credit limit.

Why do some people pay only the minimum amount due instead of making a larger payment and lowering the amount of debt they have?

When credit card companies' offer you the option of paying the minimum amount due, they are allowing you to go deeper into debt instead of helping you manage your debt. They make money when you pay interest. Making minimum payments or interest only payments, will only guarantee you will stay in debt and never get out.

Some people never realize the situation they are in and can only afford to make minimum payments. This is what I call financial slavery because debt becomes your master and you must work to pay interest or in this case less than that. Never become a slave to debt or even money. Learn to manage your income and debts properly by not spending what you cannot immediately pay off. Credit is meant to be used to be paid off in the very short term. By making long term payments on credit cards you will only make credit card companies richer, instead of helping you manage you're spending and purchases. Never choose the minimum payment option or the interest only option. Always pay down debt, even if it is by a small amount.

What do I do if I owe large amounts of money?

When you owe a lot of money in credit card debt, you need to create a plan to pay it down and stick to it until you pay it off. Some people choose to consolidate debt, while others hire a debt consolidation company. Helping yourself to be in the best possible position to pay down your debt is very important. Preparation is the key and can save you time when paying off debt.

Follow these 5 steps to prepare your credit card accounts to be paid off:

1. Call every credit card company and ask them to lower the interest rate on that card.
2. Transfer all of the debt from the higher interest rate credit cards to the lower interest rate credit cards.
3. Review your current income and expenses. Choose what expenses you currently have that can be

eliminated or reduced such as eating out, entertainment, cable bills, etc.

4. Decide what is the largest payment amount you can make towards your credit card debt based on what you currently make and find a way to increase that amount by working more hours, asking for a raise, or creating a new source of income.

5. Start paying down the credit cards that have the lowest balance as these will be the easiest to pay off first and will help you build momentum before moving to the larger balance credit cards.

When you are trying to pay off large amounts of debt, you want to start paying off the smaller balance credit cards first as this will allow you to do three very positive things. First, it will help you to create the habit of paying down debt on a monthly basis instead of carrying debt or making minimum payments. Second, it will free up cash you can now use to start paying down larger balance credit cards. Third, this will improve your credit scores which will increase your confidence to keep going. You will start to believe that what you're doing is working and this will help you to stick with the plan even if you are tempted to do otherwise.

Should I cancel or close my credit cards once I pay them off or if I am not using them at all?

Closing accounts that have a long standing credit history will hurt your credit score so make sure you consider a few more things before closing an account. Decide whether you have another account that's older than that account which will help you maintain a longer time frame of credit history. Also, consider if that account has an annual payment or additional unnecessary fees which you no longer want to make. If you can't resist getting back into debt and prefer to close it, then you should close it as it is worse to start owing money again than it is to reduce your credit history. You can always create more history over time but owing more money will mean you will get back into the habit of making minimum payments or interest-only payments.

How can I get rid of annual payments on my credit cards?

Contact the bank on your card and ask them to eliminate the annual fee or to downgrade your card so that no annual fee is charged. This option is often available as credit card companies don't want to lose you as a customer and would much rather have you keep the account open.

You can get rid of credit card annual fees by:

- Closing the card (once it's paid off!).

- Ask for the annual fee to be eliminated forever.
- Ask to have the card downgraded to a no-annual fee card.
- Ask to have the annual fee waived for that year so that you can close it when it's most convenient to you.

When do credit card companies report your payments to credit reporting agencies?

Credit card companies report your payment information every month about 30 - 45 days from the date the statement ends. They will report the amount of the payment, the new balance owed, the total credit limit and any other information that is pertinent to your account.

CHAPTER 8

How to Apply For a Credit Card and Get Approved

When you apply for a credit card, most credit card companies will review your application based on a number of factors such as: your income, your credit history, your payment history, if you have recently applied for the same card, have you been applying for other credit cards as well (too many inquiries), if you already have debts or accounts with that particular bank, if you have savings, whether you rent or own your home, etc.

Each one of these factors is an important component banks use to make the decision to grant credit or not. This is called the underwriting process. The person who underwrites your credit application is called an underwriter. They use a pre-established set of rules, also known as guidelines, to base their decision on. If you are within the guidelines, you will normally be granted credit. If you are not within the guidelines, you will receive a letter in the mail explaining why you were denied credit and where you can obtain a copy of your credit report so that you may review your credit information. There are a few cases where you might be just outside of what the guidelines allow and could receive a call from the bank where you applied for credit, as they may need to verify additional information. Talk to them and see what information they need. Sometimes it's as simple as confirming your physical address.

There are three ways to apply for a credit card:

1. Completing a physical application at the bank.
2. Completing an application over the phone by calling the bank.
3. Completing an application online.

All three are simple and easy ways to apply for a credit card. In terms of speed, online is the fastest route. If you have a bank account at that bank it can sometimes be beneficial to go to the branch since the branch representative can call the underwriter in case they have any questions or are not initialed approved. If you prefer to speak to someone over the phone make sure you are in a private space as you will be asked to provide personal information that other people should not overhear.

WHEN APPLYING FOR A CREDIT CARD MAKE SURE TO FOLLOW THESE IMPORTANT STEPS:

1. **Check your credit report before applying.** Sometimes your credit report can have inaccurate information such as the spelling of your name or your address. Other times negative information can appear that's not yours. These things need to be addressed before applying for credit as they will be reasons why you will not get approved for a credit card which can be prevented by taking action beforehand.

2. **Fill out the application completely.** People who partially complete their application are often denied or requested additional information. Sometimes credit card companies will request a copy of your identification and proof of your home address when this portion of the application is incomplete or incorrectly filled out.

3. **Make sure to use your name as it appears on your driver's license or government ID.** People who put their nicknames or middle name instead of their first

name will be denied for credit as the credit report that will be reviewed needs to match what you put on your application.

4. **Enter the total amount of your gross income** without deducting any expenses, taxes, or retirement payments. Make sure to use the total of all your income sources as this amount can include things you might forget such as: a second job, cash paid for tutoring, cleaning, summer jobs, winter jobs, online income, babysitting, etc. Having more income in relation to your expenses will benefit you when applying for credit.

5. **List all of your cash savings**. When requested to enter your checking or savings accounts, also known as liquid assets, make sure to put all of the money you have in those accounts as this too can be a reason why credit card companies will decide to approve your application.

6. **When entering your living expenses (rent or mortgage payment), make sure to be accurate with what you pay.** If you rent with two other

roommates, make sure you put what you are required to pay. If you live with a family member and don't pay rent, make sure to enter "0" or living with family or rent-free, if any of these options appear.

7. **Getting pre-approved before applying** can be a great way to see if you will be granted credit. Many credit card companies offer this option and are able to review your credit without negatively affecting your credit score. When they do this, they are able to tell you if you are pre-approved which is when you should move on towards completing the rest of the application. This can often be done in a matter of minutes through their website as credit card companies have made the application process very easy online.

8. **Employment information needs to be accurate.** Most banks want to make sure you have been in the same line of business for the past 2 years. If that's not the case, and you have only been working for 6 months, you could still get approved. Most banks just want to make sure you have an income you can use to make your payments.

9. **Don't give information you are not asked for.** Limit yourself to completing what you are asked for and not things you think you should put. If the credit card company asks for your home address, don't put you're mailing address as this could be the reason you are denied credit or receive a call from the bank in case they feel identity fraud might be taking place. Information on your credit report needs to match information on your application.

10. **Don't apply for too many credit cards all at once.** To get approved for a credit card you need to apply to the least amount of credit cards at one time. This way you won't appear to be desperately looking for credit which is a reason why some people are denied on their application. If you want to improve your credit score, you need to get approved for the credit you are applying or else you will only have credit inquiries on your credit report and no credit cards.

11. **Start with a credit card you know you will get approved for** especially if you think your credit is too new or if you have no credit at all. Some credit card companies offer secured credit cards which are accounts that require that you put a security deposit with the bank in order to be approved for the credit

card. There are also other cards which are tailored specifically to your credit rating. You can search for cards that are for bad, average, good, or even excellent credit rated customers. This way you can increase your chances of being approved and reducing the amount of credit inquiries you have in the process since you won't have to continue applying for more credit cards. If you have average credit and apply for a credit card that requires excellent credit, you will probably get denied. If you have excellent credit and apply for a credit card that requires average or good credit you will probably be approved credit. This is a smart way to approach applying for credit cards so that you match the card requirements instead of applying for what appears in the mail or for what appears on an ad.

Applying for a credit card and getting approved is more a matter of preparation than simply inputting information on a computer screen and that's the difference between getting approved or denied for credit the first time around. Be prepared by knowing where your credit stands and what your credit score is. This way you can apply for the right card. Make sure to review the application carefully and read the small print that normally goes over the interest rate and annual fees the card has. Some cards are not worth applying for simply because of all the fees you will be charged. These are the key things you need to be on the lookout when applying for a credit card.

Congratulations!

Once you have completed the steps above, you should be on your way to getting approved for a credit card.

CHAPTER 9

How to Apply For a Car Loan and Get Approved

Car loans require several things in order to get approved. While getting approved for a credit card is easier than getting approved for a car loan, there are things you can do to make it easier.

Car loans are secured by the car you're buying so banks will look at your credit as the borrower and the car as well. If you are buying a car that's worth less than the loan you're getting, you might not get approved so you want to make sure the price is reasonable and you're not overpaying.

If you have never purchased a car before, you might be asked to put a down payment in order to get approved for the car loan. The more down payment you put, the easier it is to get approved.

While the application and approval process might be lengthy, make sure not to rush through the process. Read everything carefully to prevent making mistakes that could cause you to be denied or give you a lot more work than is normally necessary.

WHEN APPLYING FOR A CAR LOAN YOU NEED TO MAKE SURE TO FOLLOW THESE IMPORTANT STEPS:

1. **Make sure your employer is aware they might receive a phone call from the bank.** Most banks will call to verify you work in the position you put in the application and for the length of time you stated. Make sure you put this information along with your income correctly. Also, double check the phone number you enter so that the right department answers the phone which should normally be the human resource department for your employer. Don't risk having the front desk put the bank on hold indefinitely.

2. **Check your credit report to make sure your name and address are accurate** so that you enter the same information on the credit application. If the information on the application does not match, you will be asked to provide additional proof in the form of a cell phone bill, utility bill, driver's license or similar id that shows your home address.

3. **Check your credit scores before going to the dealer.** Often times, making payments on time should mean having a high credit score but that's not always the case. In some cases, you can have an average credit score even though you make payments on time due to other reasons such as: short payment history, too many credit inquiries, too little available credit, etc. Having credit scores above 700 is a good thing. Having credit scores below 620 is a bad thing and will often require you to make a down payment in order to get approved for a car loan.

4. **Your living history needs to be accurate** and needs to complete a 2 year length which is what most banks need to verify when reviewing a credit application. If you lived for 1 year at one residence and 3 years at another, you need to specify the amount of time for each one in order to prevent the bank from denying you credit. It doesn't matter if you have been living with your family, renting, or paying a mortgage as long as you can provide 2 years of living history. This is not a requirement but it will allow you to get approved with the least down payment and less restrictions. Not having 2 years of living history will not get you denied but it's a good thing to have when applying.

5. **Past car loans that have been paid on time or even paid off** are very positive things banks want to see on your credit report as this will help them make a decision. Showing a track record of making payments on time in general will always be viewed as a sign of stability by banks. It normally means you have had an income and a job. Being able to manage money properly and making payments on time go hand in hand.

6. **Negative credit information will require that you show a recent history of payments made on time.** If you had a late payment 2 years ago but made payments on time after that, it will be a sign of recent payment stability on your part. On the other hand, if you had a late payment a month or two ago, you will probably be offered a higher interest rate or be required to put some form of down payment. Make sure you get your credit history in order and make consistent payments for at least a year before you consider applying for a car loan. This way, you will allow yourself to be in a better negotiating position when trying to get the lowest monthly payment.

7. **Proof of cash savings might be useful when applying for a car** loan at times. When banks go over your income, they might see that it is too low and will need to find a way to qualify you for the loan by using your cash reserves. This does not mean banks will use your savings as a down payment, it simply means that they may ask you to verify if you have enough savings in case your income is not sufficient to make future payments. You can provide the bank with your most recent bank statement showing enough cash reserves.

8. **Apply for a car loan with a bank you already have accounts with.** This will definitely increase your chances of getting approved for a car loan as most banks work hard to sell customers as many of their products as possible to maintain customer loyalty. This is called cross-selling. Most banks feel more comfortable lending to a current bank customer than a new one when both financial conditions are compared. Always ask the dealer to provide you with the necessary documentation to give to your bank so they may qualify you and the car. They may need to confirm that you are not financing a car that is worth much less than what you are paying. You will be surprised to see that your bank will be very

motivated to help you and will usually offer competitive rates and terms.

9. **Always rate shop other credit unions and community banks** as they are always looking to grant credit worthy customers a car loan. These types of lending institutions often have special rate discounts and offers on loans that will benefit you. Some even offer to let you start making your first payments 60 to 90 days from when the application is approved which can be very convenient.

Congratulations!

Once you have completed the steps above, you should be on your way to getting approved for a car loan.

CHAPTER 10

How to Apply For a Mortgage and Get Approved

When applying for a mortgage you need to prepare your finances and your credit beforehand. Having good credit history will increase your chances of being approved. An accurately completed loan application is essential so that the bank representative that makes the final decision (underwriter), can approve you for a loan. Most mortgage applications are long but will provide the bank with a complete overview of your current financial situation and your overall credit worthiness. Most banks want to give you a mortgage but have to follow a specific set of rules called guidelines. These guidelines need to be followed when approving a loan.

In general, there are six things that need to happen for you to own a home:

- Get prequalified by a bank.
- Find the home you want to purchase.
- Apply for financing (unless you're paying cash.)
- Get approved by the bank.

- Close on the loan by signing all mortgage and legal papers as well as bringing the bank required down payment funds.
- Move into your new home.

The primary people involved in the home purchase process

For these six things to happen you will need different people to do their job. These are the people that are normally involved in the home purchasing process:

- Loan officer (The bank or mortgage company representative who takes your application.)
- Processor (The bank representative who processes your loan.)
- Underwriter (The bank representative who determines if you are approved or denied for the loan.)
- Realtor (The person who helps you to find your home, prepare the contract, and negotiates with the seller's realtor on your behalf.)
- Appraiser (The person who appraises the value of the home you are buying.)
- Surveyor (The person who determines the homes boundaries and other spaces around the home.)

- Title agent (A title company representative who verifies ownership of the property and completes other title related due diligence.)
- Closing agent (The person who explains and has you sign all legal documentation at the closing pertaining to the purchase of your home. This can often be the title agent as well.)

Get prequalified or pre-approved

Getting pre-approved before searching for a home is the best way to start so that you know exactly what home prices you should be looking for. You don't want to find the perfect home and then find out you don't qualify for that purchase price. You can get pre-approved by a bank loan officer or a mortgage representative by contacting them and completing a loan application. They will check your credit and review your financial information.

Find a realtor

If it's your first time purchasing a home, it would be better if you found an experienced realtor to walk you through the process once you have been prequalified by the bank. This will save you time and potential problems. Realtors have access to current homes for sale in the area where you are looking to buy.

IN GENERAL, MOST BANKS WILL REQUIRE THE FOLLOWING THINGS IN ORDER TO APPROVE YOUR LOAN:

A minimum credit score is necessary. For some banks it may be as low as 580 while for others this number can be as high as 700. Most banks will give you a better rate when you have a higher credit score. All banks check all three credit scores for each credit bureau: Experian®, Transunion®, and Equifax®. From these three numbers they choose the middle score to make a decision. For example, if you have these three credit scores: 683 702 733

Your bank would use the 702 score to decide what your rate would be and to determine other risk based factors which basically means how risky you are as a borrower.

Make sure to check your credit scores from each one of the credit bureaus to make sure you have good enough credit scores.

Minimum credit history is important for banks to see if you have paid on time and for how long. When you have no credit history, it's difficult to determine if you will pay on time in the future if approved for a mortgage.

Sufficient income is necessary to be approved for a loan. Based on the income you provide, the bank will calculate up to what amount of a loan you would qualify for. Your total gross income is used to calculate what you qualify for. Your total gross income is the total income you make before any deductions. Net income is what you actually deposit in your bank account.

Gross income: $5,000 (This number is used to qualify you for a mortgage.)

Net income: $4,300 (This is what you actually receive after all deductions in the form of income.)

Total expenses are calculated using your credit report. Your total expenses are calculated by simply adding up all the payments you make that appear on your credit report.

For example:

Credit card payments: $300

Car loan payment: $330

Store card payment: $50

Total expenses would be: $680

$300 + $330 + $50 = $680

Total household expenses are calculated by adding the payments that appear on your credit report and the new total mortgage payments you will have once you own the home. Your total mortgage payments will include: principal and interest, taxes, insurance, homeowners association dues (if applicable), and mortgage insurance if you are required to have it. If you put less than 20% down payment, you will be required by the bank to have mortgage insurance.

For example:

Total expenses: $700

Total mortgage payments: $1,750

Total household expenses: $2,450

$700 + $1,750 = $2,450

Your debt to income ratio is calculated to determine if you are within the bank approved guidelines. These vary depending on the loan program but normally must be at least below 50%. The debt to income ratio is calculated by dividing your total household expenses by your total gross income.

For example:

If your total gross income is $5,000 and your total household expenses are $2,000, you're debt to income ratio would be 0.40 or 40%. If you are below 50%, you may qualify for some loan programs. Ideally, you want to be below 41%.

$2,000/$5,000 = 40% debt to income ratio

Total liquid assets are important when deciding to approve your loan or not. Your assets are all the things you have of value but for mortgage purposes, the ones you have in the form of cash in a bank account that can be used for future payments and for a down payment.

For example:

If the bank requires that you have enough money for a 5% down payment and 4 months of payment reserves, you would need to have these funds available in your bank account:

Purchase price: $300,000

5% down payment: $15,000

$300,000 X 0.05 = $15,000

Total monthly mortgage payment: $2,400

4 months payment reserves: $9,600

$2,400 X 4 = $9,600

5% down payment plus 4 months' payment reserves: $24,600

$15,000 + $9,600 = $24,600 total funds available in a bank account to be approved by the bank for the loan, of which only $15,000 will be used for the purchase since the 4 months reserves only need to show in your bank account.

The down payment can sometimes come from a family member in the form of a gift which can often lower what you need to have in your bank account to be approved by the bank. There are also down payment assistance programs if you don't have sufficient down payment funds.

NOTE: You will additionally need money for closing costs which can sometimes be financed by the seller and other times will need to be paid by you at closing. Make sure to ask for the total closing costs after you have applied for a loan (it should show in your loan estimate) so that you have a general idea of what you will need to have in your bank account for closing costs in addition to the down payment and the reserves as the bank will require that you have this amount before closing.

A minimum of two years in the same line of work is necessary to get approved. Sometimes in certain professions there are exceptions to this rule. You can have worked as a nurse in one hospital and moved to another one within two years and still be approved for a loan since you continued to work as a nurse even if you were employed by two different hospitals.

A minimum of two years of living history needs to be provided. Banks just want to confirm two years' worth of living history. It does not matter if you lived with family or if you rented, as long as you can provide all addresses where you have lived in the past two years.

Congratulations!

Once you have these things approved and your credit history and scores are sufficient, you should be on your way to getting approved for a home loan.

CHAPTER 11

How to Qualify For Credit When You Have No Credit At All

Most people who don't have credit still have alternatives to creating credit rather quickly using a number of different methods. Let's go over some of your options.

Getting a secured loan

Secured loans are easy to get as long as you have cash available to put up as a guarantee. Secured credit cards are a fast alternative that can be opened with very low initial amounts. Often, you can start with a $300 or $500 credit limit which will increase over time and as long as you make payments on time which is the whole purpose of applying for these types of credit cards. You will be required to deposit the same amount for which you are being granted credit into a specific bank account which will serve as collateral. Once you pay on time for at least 3 to 6 months, your credit report should start showing a history of payments which will allow you to have a credit score which is essential when applying for other loans will be easier. Once you have a credit score above 640 or 660 you can apply for another credit card that isn't require to be secured with your cash. If you are approved for the new credit card you can go ahead and close the secured credit card account and receive your cash deposit back. This is a process but it works well and creates credit within a few months.

CD secured loans are also another option when trying to create credit. You will basically go to a bank that offers CD (certificate of deposit) secured loans and ask them what their minimum amount to open is to apply for a CD secured loan and if any fees will be charged in the process. You will end up depositing a specific amount. Try to keep it as low as possible since you always want to have cash savings available for every day expenses and unexpected emergencies. You will receive a loan in exchange for the cash you put in the CD which will need to be paid back on a monthly basis. The shorter the term of the loan and the CD, the better as you don't want to tie up your money for too long. Once you pay off the loan and the CD matures, you can close the loan and the CD so that you get your money back.

Authorized signer

Ask a friend or family member to add you as an authorized signer on their credit card account. This will allow you to have credit history in a matter of a month or two since you will have all the credit history that your friend or family member has on their account. Make sure they have paid on time and will continue doing so or else you will start off with bad credit which is not the goal. All it takes is a phone call by your friend or family member asking to have you added as an authorized signer on their card. They will receive a card for you in the mail and they can choose if they want you to have access to the card or not. This way they can limit their risk in case they don't feel comfortable giving you access to their credit card but still want to help.

Joint signer or Co-signer

Asking someone else to co-sign on a loan or credit card is a great way to be granted credit as long as payments are made on time. You never want to ask someone else to help you get accepted for credit and then make late payments which would negatively affect both of your credit scores. As long as they have good enough credit, you will both be granted credit. When you are just starting to build credit, having a co-signer will be very helpful.

If you have to choose between being an authorized signer or having a co-signer choose the authorized signer option as to minimize your friend or family members risk.

Apply for a car loan

Car loans are one of the easiest loans to get approved for. Sometimes you will have higher interest rates and may be required to put a down payment but it will be well worth it. You will be able to build credit with every payment you make and will be able to apply for other forms of credit successfully thanks to the credit history you will be creating. Banks know the loan is being secured by a car so they feel more comfortable granting credit. You might still need to have a co-signer to get approved for a car loan but if you want to get a loan by yourself you may have to put up a larger down payment and might have a higher interest rate. If you don't want to have a high interest rate for too long you always have other options such as: refinancing your car loan, trading it in for another car once you see your credit report shows consistent payments made on time, sell the car, or pay off the car once you have built sufficient credit.

Student loan

Apply for a student loan if you are planning to go to school. You don't need to apply for a large amount. You just need to get approved for the loan and then pay it back on time. This is can be a longer process than some of the other options shown when trying to create credit but it's still another option. If you are not planning on going to school, don't apply for a student loan just to create credit.

Rent and utility bills

Your rental payment and utility bills will not show up on your credit report on their own but you can always request that they reflect on your credit. Ask your landlord to reflect your positive payment history on your credit report which will immediately create credit history and a credit score. You can also provide all three of the credit bureaus copies of your utility bills and have them verify payment history so that you create a positive credit history without incurring any debts. Utility bills can include: electricity, gas, water, and even cell phone payments in some cases.

These are all valid options when trying to credit history. Not all of them will apply to you but some will and can be very beneficial. Remember, you are making an investment in your credit so that you can get better financing terms in the future which could save you thousands over time. If you are considering to purchase a home, make sure you have established considerable positive payment history so that you are approved and have reasonable rates and terms.

CHAPTER 12

Real Life Example of Someone Who Increased Their Credit Score to Over 800 Starting From Having No Credit At All

For some people it can be a slow and difficult process when trying to increase your credit score but with proper planning and some creative solutions, you can bring your score up.

This is the story of Jamie. Jamie had no credit and no credit score. She now has an 803 credit score. She learned not to force credit but to manage debt wisely. She didn't accumulate very much debt and never had more than one type of credit account (credit cards). Most people think they need to have a credit card, store card, car loan, and a mortgage to have a high credit score but this is a contradiction as you will see in Jamie's story. This might work for some people but not for others. Let's go over Jamie's situation to see how she was able to make this happen.

Jamie's story

Jamie came from abroad and had no credit or debts in her name. Her credit report was blank.

Her husband had her added as an authorized signer on one of his credit cards instead of applying for a secured credit card. This had a positive effect after just a couple months since her credit report now showed a 667 credit score and the credit card reflected a history of positive on-time payments. She decided to apply for a credit card but was declined since she mistakenly applied for a credit card that required a 700 credit score. Even though it's never a good thing to be denied credit, it was a good lesson. After her husband made payments on time for 6 months on the credit card Jamie was an authorized signer on which reflected on her credit report, Jamie applied for a credit card that required only a 660 credit score so she was immediately approved a credit card with a $5,000 credit limit. She charged a small amount of $44 on it and then made a payment in full so no debt was owed on it. After 6 months, she applied for another credit card that required a 700 credit score and offered a bonus of 50,000 miles when spending $3,500 within 3 months. This was a good option since many payments needed to be made at home which would allow them to cover the required $3,500 in spending. They charged their car insurance, cell phone payments, and other expenses every month and once they reached $3,500 they stopped using that credit card. The following month they paid off that card in full but did not close it. Her credit score jumped to over 714. She repeated this process with two other hotel points and bonus cash back credit card offers which increased her credit score to over 756 within the next two years. For the next year, she only used those cards for small purchases which were immediately paid off in full so no debt was carried from month to month.

Even though applying for different credit cards meant having inquiries appear on her credit report, they were all approved except for one so far. This was because she stopped applying for credit cards which she knew she would not get approved for which was very smart. She also did not carry large amounts of debt from month to month which meant she kept her debt to credit limit ratios very low or even at "0". She did not keep applying for credit every month.

After making payments on a consistent basis and paying off in full any credits cards that had a balance for over a year, her credit score bumped again to 803. She had a positive payment history for an extended period of time. After just 5 years of being granted credit, she had an over 800 credit score.

How was Jamie viewed by banks and lenders?

Because Jamie did not carry debt, she didn't appear to be in financial trouble and showed responsible spending habits which is one of the main things all banks want to see. She didn't keep applying for credit cards she did not need so she did not appear to be desperately in need of money. Jamie appeared as a great borrower to many banks.

How is Jamie different from other borrowers?

Jamie only had credit cards and did not carry debt for over 2 or 3 months. Most of the time she paid them off the following month so she didn't make interest payments. Jamie also did not apply constantly for credit or for credit she knew she would be denied. Most people carry debt from month to month and have too many credit cards. They owe a large percentage of what they have available on their credit limits. Most people have other types of credit they sometimes don't need.

Learning from Jamie's experience

Jamie's situation might not apply to everyone but it's a true story of someone who increased their credit score passed 800 by managing only credit card debt in a smart and patient manner. You can do the same if you follow a similar path.

CREDIT SCORE MYTHS

Most people think certain things need to happen to have a great credit score. Most of these myths are wrong and affect their potential to have the highest score possible. Knowing what is true and what is a myth could save you years of mismanaged credit. Focus on reality and not on myths by going over some of the most common misconceptions shown below:

If you're 21 years of age or younger, you can't have a credit score above 700

Wrong. Your credit score is not age based and it does not take this criteria into account when calculating your score.

If I get married, my credit score will go down

Wrong, your credit score is independent to your spouse's score unless you have joint credit accounts in which case payment history and the amount of debt carried can affect you in a positive or negative manner. Your marital status is irrelevant.

If I pay off all my credit cards I will have an 800 credit score

Incorrect. Paying off your credit cards should increase your credit score but there are more factors to take into account when determining your credit score such as: length of credit history, credit mix, inquiries, debt capacity, etc.

If I check my credit online, it will go down

There are times when having your credit checked or when you check your credit that you're credit scores will not be affected. Normally, your credit score is affected when you apply for credit and your credit is pulled, not when you check your own credit.

If I lose my job, my score will go down

This is not correct. Your employment status is not linked to your credit and will not affect your credit score. If you are late on payments as a result of losing your job, this will result in a lower score. If you can keep making your payments on time your score will not go down.

If I make a million dollars a year, I will have a credit score above 750

No. Your credit scores are not affected by how much you make. Your salary can be $100 or $1,000,000, your score will not change. Managing your credit properly will affect your credit. Some people that are very wealthy can have low credit scores while someone who is getting paid minimum wage can have an over 800 credit score.

If I buy a house worth $700,000 and owe $600,000 my credit will be negatively affected because of the amount of debt I owe

This is not correct. Applying for a mortgage will lower your credit scores because they are being pulled to review your credit but the amount you owe is irrelevant. Your monthly payment can be $4,000 on your mortgage and your credit will not be affected. Once you start paying down your $600,000 loan, your credit will improve as a result of paying on time and lowering you debt. If you put 10% or 30% down payment on a house you buy, your credit will not be affected by this either since it is payment history based and will only be affected by your capacity to repay the loan.

If I move to another country my credit score will go down

It does not matter where you live, credit history and your credit score is based on your capacity to manage debt properly not on where you are. You can live in New York City, Miami, Seattle, Washington D.C., Los Angeles, Mexico, Germany, Australia, and your credit score will not be affected.

If I turn 80 years old I will no longer be able to improve my credit score

Wrong, age is not a factor when it comes to your credit and your credit score. If you live to be 120 years old, you can continue having great credit and a high credit score.

If I make a late payment on my credit card my score will drop to 300

Incorrect, assuming a score based on a late payment is not the way to assess your credit score as it can be slightly lower or it can drop much lower. There is no precise way to know exactly what your score will be.

If I apply for too many credit cards my score will go down

Correct. Credit inquiries lower your credit score by a small amount but when you continually apply for credit, your credit will be checked often and will result in a lower score.

CREDIT VOCABULARY

Authorized signer: someone who is able to make purchases on an account but is not legally liable for the owing balance.

Bankruptcy chapter 7: is a court process that allows an individual to get rid of all liability on personal debt.

Bankruptcy chapter 13: is a court process that allows a person to eliminate some debts, reduce monthly payments on certain debts, and catch up on mortgage payments.

Bankruptcy chapter 11: is a court process that allows a corporation to propose a reorganization of debt payments to its creditors.

Car loan: is a way to finance the purchase of an automobile where principal and interest payments are normally paid over a fixed period of time.

CD secured loan: is a loan made by a bank or lending institution that is secured or backed by a certificate of deposit.

Co-signer: is a person who is responsible for paying back a loan along with another person or persons.

Credit bureau: is a company that collects information that is relevant to your credit and has been provided by other financial and non-financial institutions.

Credit card: is a plastic card used to make purchases on credit.

Credit history: is the accumulation of data on a borrowers past repayment of debts provided from different sources including, lending institutions, banks, government agencies, collection agencies, etc.

Credit report: is a report that explains in detail a borrower's credit history.

Credit score: is a number assigned to determine a person's credit worthiness based on an analysis of their credit history and debt management.

Debt collection: is a debt that has been sent to a third party debt collector. They will normally use all legal means to collect an unpaid debt.

Derogative credit: are all items that have shown a negative history of debt repayment, including: late payments, collections, bankruptcies, etc.

Experian: is one of the main credit reporting agencies that provides many different credit products. It is commonly known to report a borrower's credit history and provide this report, upon request, to the borrower or creditors.

Equifax: is one of the largest credit reporting agencies in the U.S. that reports a borrower's credit history. It provides this report, upon request, to the borrower or creditors.

FICO score: is a type of credit score that details a borrower's credit history so that creditors may assess the level of risk when determining to grant a loan or not.

Hard inquiry: is when a lender checks your credit report before making the decision to grant credit. All three credit scores are normally pulled.

Mortgage: is a binding legal agreement between a borrower and a lender where the lender lends money at a specific interest in exchange for taking title of the debtor's property.

Late payment: is a payment that is made after an agreed payment date set forth by the credit grantor. Normally a fixed payment date is provided in advance.

Secured credit card: is a loan that is secured by a cash collateral deposit which becomes a credit line for the credit card account.

Soft inquiry: is when a person or financial institution pulls your credit report with the purpose of granting a loan.

Student loan: is a type of loan used by students to pay for school. This type of loan is normally used when starting post-secondary education.

Transunion: is one of three of the largest credit reporting agencies in the United States that reports a borrower's credit history. It provides this report, upon request, to the borrower or creditors.